Where Is the Butterfly?

Seed Learning

ant

butterfly

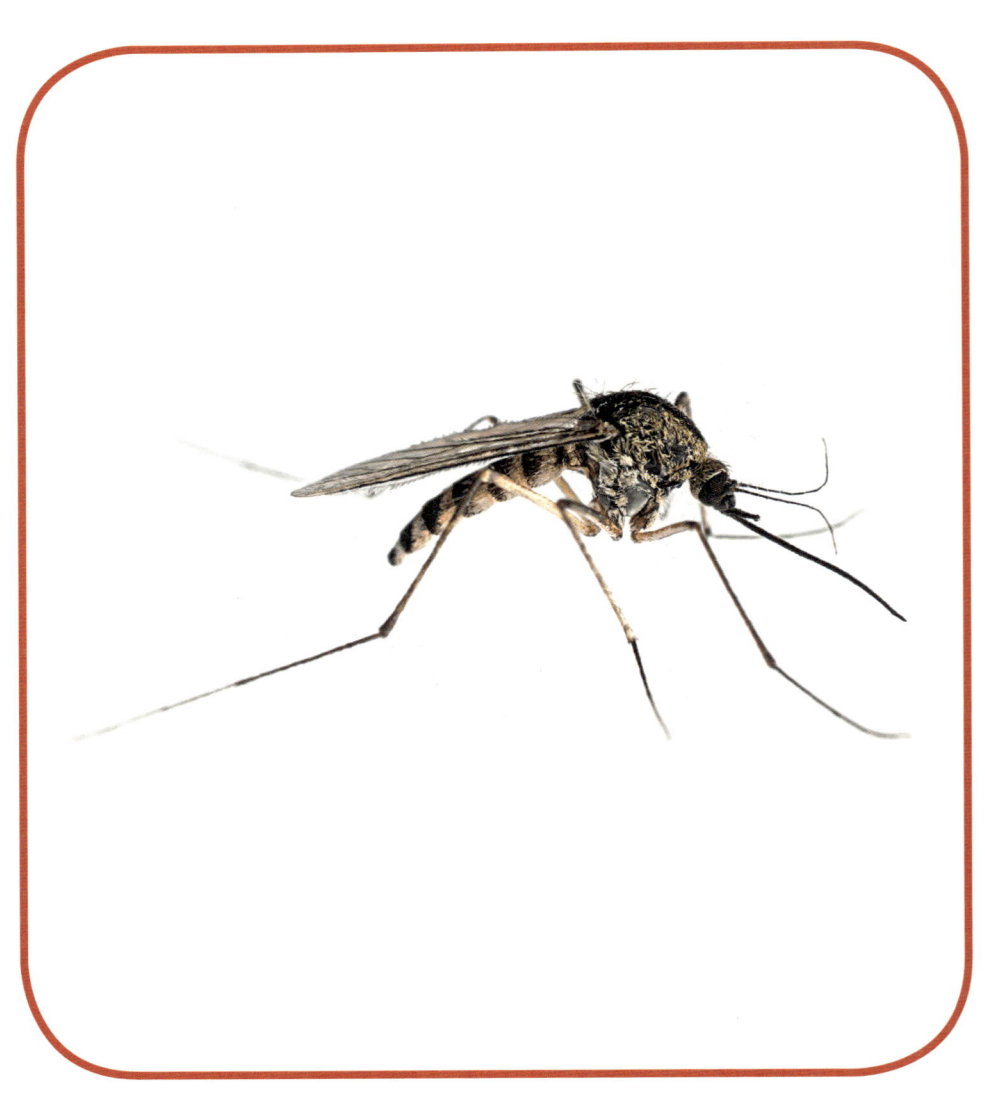

mosquito

snail

spider

beetle

ladybug

dragonfly

Where is
the butterfly?

Here it is.

Where is
the snail?

Here it is.

Where is the ladybug?

Here it is.

Where is the dragonfly?

Here it is.

Where is the spider?

Here it is.

Where is
the mosquito?

Oh, no! Here it is!

Let's learn about New Zealand.

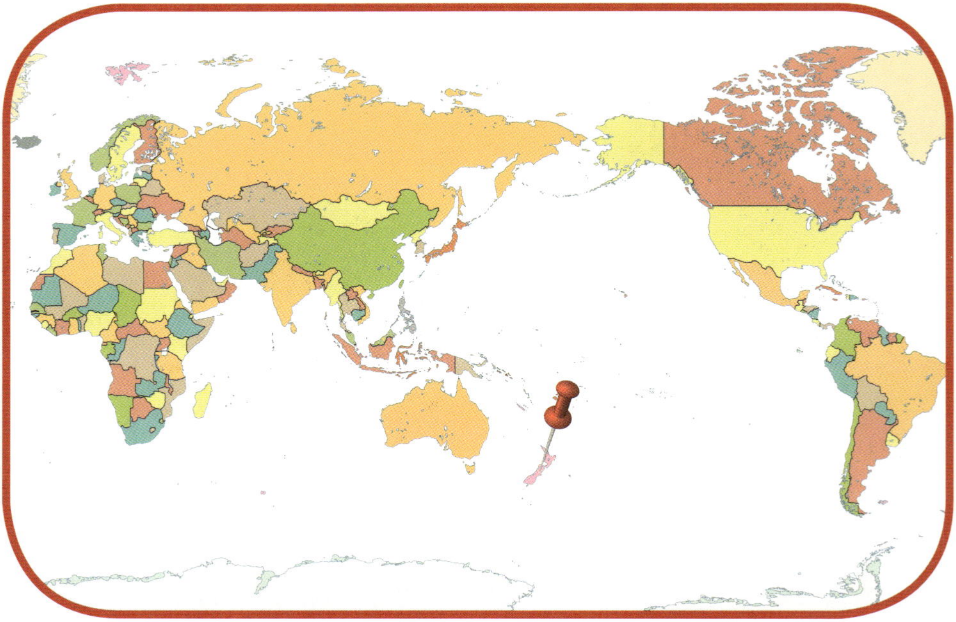

Flag of New Zealand

One Tree Hill